# The Big Book of Recovery Poems

# The Big Book of Recovery Poems

Yvonne Stringer

Rev. date: 06/30/2015

**To order additional copies of this book, contact:**
Xlibris
1-888-795-4274
www.Xlibris.com
Orders@Xlibris.com
717958

# CONTENTS

## THE BATTLES FOR LIFE

## THE BATTLES OF ADDICTION

## THE BATTLES FOR HAPPINESS

# Introduction

Many people struggle with feeling alone in their addiction. Some may feel no one can relate to what they went through or feel there is no hope. Others may be too proud to ask for help. Admitting that you have a problem is the first step to becoming the new you. This is a book of hope, strength, struggle and recovery. These poems were written while I was in a treatment facility battling my very own addiction, fighting for my life. While addiction is a very trying time in anyone's life, there is someone out there willing to lend a listening ear so you don't have to fight alone. These poems have inspired many men and women and hopefully will continue to inspire many more. From growing up as an isolated child to surviving domestic violence, The Big Book of Recovery Poems is here to instill comfort and the message to the addict who feels there is no future for them. So for the addict sitting in treatment facilities, living rooms, libraries, work places, institutions and shelters, I believe in you. It's so much freedom in the choices you make. I challenge you to make one that turns you into a happier, honest, caring person. You have the power to change your life RIGHT NOW.

Enjoy your read.

# The Battles for Life

# Just Wait

You don't know what it's like
To be trapped inside one's self

You're like a doll who sits
Upon one's shelf

Never to move
In all your days of glory

Nothing to do
But to look, cry and worry

Head pointed forward
Back stuck straight

Can't move a muscle
Can't scream
Just wait…

# Do I Look Happy?

Do I look happy to you?
I bet you think I do
But inside it's a raging storm
Scattered pieces of paper torn
From here to there
To everywhere
You think it's fun to be me?
Just wait until you see the things I see
My hands are shaking right now
I want to scream but I don't know how
So much anger is furling inside
But happiness and sunshine shows outside
This beast will not be contained
These tears in my eyes will not rain
My breathing is heavy. My breathing is hard
Why did I have to be dealt this card?
The words form in my brain
My heart is so full of pain
I can't seem to say what's in my head
My thoughts won't go away if I'm dead
The noise all around I don't want to hear
Being judged is my greatest fear
I'm afraid of what others might say
That's why I don't trust people to this day
Who are you to talk?
You can't fill the shoes in which I walk
So again I ask, "Do I look happy to you?"
On the outside I bet you think that I do...

# *Strength*

When I think about what you did to me
My life was in turmoil, it was plain to see
All the fighting and all the bruises
All the lies and all the excuses
I didn't deserve it that I know
I should have left a long time ago
I was stuck; had low self-esteem
On me you let out your steam
Every night I cried to sleep
Trying to be quiet and not make a peep
Waking up without knowing
Which way the day would be going
When I brush my hair, it starts to shed
Will this be the day they find me dead?
All the time I was hurting inside
While you walked around with so much pride
You thought I was weak and so did I
I thought I was alone so I didn't even try
But up until yesterday
I realized I had another way
I can take my power and control
Erase the thoughts you try to hold
Because I am beautiful. I am strong
Everything you told me was all wrong.

# *Memories*

I'll never forget the things
You put me through
I remember when my eyes
Were black and blue

Spitting in my face
Calling me names
I was so sick and tired
Of playing those games

I thank God everyday
For sparing my life
I don't know what I would've done
If I had become your wife

If I saw you
The day after forever
It would be too soon
I'd prefer never!

# Too Busy to Die

*I just picked up the pen*
*And decided to write*
*I guess I had trouble*
*Sleeping last night*

*You see everyday*
*Thoughts come to past*
*About whether or not*
*I want my life to last*

*I contemplate suicide*
*Quite a lot now*
*I stare into space*
*Trying to figure out how*

*The good news with death*
*Is that once it's over*
*I'll no longer have to worry*
*About being sober*

*There's just one problem*
*With that idea of mine*
*It seems to be*
*I just haven't the time.*

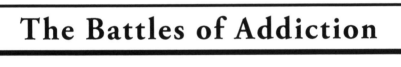

# The Battles of Addiction

# With These Hands

Day in and day out
I look at these hands
Thinking of things
I don't understand
With these hands
I've done so much
Only to my kids
A gentle touch
Hands around necks
Hands around throats
Every night
Terrors I awoke
Remembering events
That kept me using
With these hands
I kept abusing
I took my hands
I picked up drugs
That was passed out
By neighborhood thugs
So what I must do
Is take these hands
Fight for my life
And take a stand
I look at these hands
I know I'm tough
My life's not easy
But it's not rough

# Enemy

*Talk to me*
*Just say my name*
*Open up a little*
*Just play my game*

*Hop on the rollercoaster*
*I won't make you sick*
*Buckle up*
*I'll show you a trick*

*Close your eyes*
*Think of me*
*Open them*
*What do you see?*

*If you want bad teeth*
*Or bad breath*
*Pick me up*
*I'll carry you to death*

*I'll whisper to you*
*Sing you a song*
*I'll keep your secret*
*Tell me what's wrong*

Lay with me
I'll keep you warm
Hold me close
I mean you no harm

Close your fist
Keep it tight
I won't hurt
Don't try to fight

I'll never go away
I think you know
When you least expect it
I'll start to show

Crawling at
The back of your mind
I'll snatch at you
Get you from behind

You belong to me
I thought you knew
You went to rehab
You thought you grew

*That alone*
*Won't help now*
*Won't let go*
*No way no how*

*Keep it up*
*Keep going back*
*I won't release*
*I'll throw you off track*

*I had you before*
*I'll have you again*
*Twelve steps won't work*
*I'm in for the win*

*That sponsor's a lie*
*Not telling the truth*
*I'll wait for you*
*I'll sit on your stoop*

*I'm waiting for you*
*Can't you see?*
*Don't you dare*
*Give up on me!*

*I'll gain your attention*
*I'm always right*
*Here in the dark*
*Get out of the light*

*All the time*
*Day after day*
*You study your book*
*What does it say?*

*Put it down*
*It's no good*
*Come on let's go*
*Ride to the hood*

*All your friends*
*Are waiting for you*
*You know what I'm saying*
*It's all true*

*When you give up*
*I'll see you around*
*I won't give up*
*I'm right underground*

*When you get hurt*
*Sad or depressed*
*Just lay back*
*I'll help you rest*

*God has you now*
*But in due time*
*You'll feel hurt*
*Then you'll be mine*

*I bet you think*
*I'll let you be*
*I can't do that*
*I'm your enemy.*

# My Enemy

I talked to you
I said your name
I opened up
I played your game

I got on the rollercoaster
Yeah, you made a sick
I buckled up
Yeah, you played a trick

I closed my eyes
I thought of you
I opened them
But you wasn't true

I love my teeth
I love my health
You won't have the
Satisfaction of my death

I blocked you out
When you sung me a song
You told me lies
And you were wrong

*I stayed with you*
*You showed your charm*
*You hurt my body*
*You did me harm*

*I opened my hand*
*And in plain sight*
*You tried to hold on*
*With all of your might*

*I pushed you away*
*I think you see*
*You didn't expect it*
*At least from me*

*You crawled in*
*The back of my thoughts*
*You thought I was*
*Bruised, broken, distraught*

*I belong to God*
*He's my priest*
*All your antics*
*Are hereby ceased*

That in itself
Does truly show
Which way my Father
Wants me to go

I plan to keep it up
I will go back
So get your things
You've got to pack

You had me once
But not anymore
I have chosen
To close that door

My sponsor's a help
She does care
You can wait all you want
But I won't be there

You can look for me
But I'm hard to find
I had to choose
To leave you behind

I don't pay you attention
You get on my nerves
God gave you exactly
What you deserve

*Oh, yes everyday*
*I'm in my book*
*Trying to correct*
*The road I took*

*I won't put it down*
*I won't put it away*
*Away from my book*
*I will not stray*

*They weren't my friends*
*They can't hold my hand*
*I put on my armor*
*Against you I must stand*

*I won't give up*
*You won't see me around*
*For all I care*
*You can stay underground*

*Yes, I'll get hurt*
*I might even cry*
*But I'll turn to the one*
*Who is Most High*

*Yes, God has me now*
*My heart he does hold*
*When you come around*
*I'll do as I'm told*

*I bet you thought*
*I'd let you be*
*I couldn't do that*
*You're my enemy...*

# The Hustle

*Being Out in the streets*
*Naw, it ain't a joke*
*Hustling hard*
*Don't wanna be broke*

*Getting what I wanted*
*That was my art*
*Stealing from stores*
*Put it right in the cart*

*Walking the streets*
*In the dead of the night*
*Dealing with jerks*
*Who put up a fight*

*All I wanted*
*Was a lot of money*
*But they made it hard*
*For people like me*

*It's hard sometimes*
*When you don't have a job*
*I'm tired of doing this*
*I don't want to rob*

*Selling my body*
*Never felt good*
*Didn't think in all my life*
*That I ever would*

*I got what I needed*
*I got what I wanted*
*And if I got you*
*In your face I'd still flaunt it*

*You could never see*
*The things I saw*
*The streets ain't no joke*
*Man, the streets are raw*

*Catchin' people off guard*
*Catchin' people slippin'*
*Can't believe I did that*
*Man, I was trippin'*

*Any one of them*
*Could've shot me dead*
*It would only take*
*One bullet to the head*

*I can't go around*
*Playing with people's lives*
*Hittin' their nest*
*Stirrin' up beehives*

*I have to fix my life*
*I wanna get it straight*
*Have my own things*
*Wouldn't that be great*

*I'm gonna make it*
*That I know*
*So stand back*
*And watch me grow*

*I bury that life*
*It's no longer mine*
*The rain has stopped*
*Here comes sunshine*

# Addiction

My mouth was dry
My hands were sweaty
My clothes were dirty
Somehow I was still ready

Ready for what
I wasn't really sure
My life back then
Was much of a blur

Not taking a shower
Not going to sleep
Not combing my hair
Not much to eat

Oh, those were the days
In my addiction
I'd lost so much
To my own affliction

I couldn't see past
That very next hit
I wandered about
To see what I could get

*I was losing my family*
*I was losing my friends*
*I was leading my life*
*To the bitter end*

*I had to find hope*
*I had to find courage*
*I couldn't give up*
*I couldn't be discouraged*

*I've been through a lot*
*But I am still here*
*So with that I say*
*I shall have nothing to fear!*

# The Battles for Happiness

# Define Happy

Define happy
What does it mean?
In your eye
There's a little gleam

Define happy
What's it to you?
Make it through the day
Without feeling blue?

Define happy
How does it feel?
Can you touch it?
Is it truly real?

Define happy
Is it just a thought?
Or as a kid,
Is it taught?

Define happy
Does it travel through the air?
Is it honest?
Is it even fair?

*Define happy*
*Is it you? Is it me?*
*Something we can smell?*
*Something we can see?*

*Define happy*
*Is it good? Is it bad?*
*Does it make you feel good?*
*Does it make you feel sad?*

*Define happy*
*Oh, if I did such a thing*
*I'd tell you that happy*
*Is a song only you can sing.*

# A Kid Again

The world is my playground
I have so much fun
Just running around in circles
Under the afternoon sun

Swinging on the swing
Sliding down the slide
Playing Hide & Seek
Having to run and hide

Playing Eenie Meenie
Miney Moe
S.O.S
And Tic Tac Toe

Climbing trees
Swimming in pools
Staying up late
When there is no school

Laughing at my friends
When they make funny faces
Playing lots of Kickball
Having lots of races

*Flying kites*
*High in the sky*
*Not a care in the world*
*Never wondering why*

*Chasing the Popsicle truck*
*Just for a lollipop*
*You only have a quarter*
*But you still hope he'll stop*

*Chewing Jumbo Gumballs*
*Putting on a fake tattoo*
*Making your skin peel*
*When you added a lot of glue*

*I had so much fun*
*When I was a little kid*
*All the things I wanted*
*To do, I did*

*Yeah, there was good*
*There was also bad*
*Times I was happy*
*And times I was sad*

*For better or for worse*
*That was my life*
*Take it or leave it*
*But I wouldn't think twice…*

# Dream, Baby, Dream

When I was a girl, I didn't dream
I didn't dream at all
When I thought of what I wanted
My thoughts came to a stall

I thought of being a teacher
Help the little kids
All I did was act out
That's exactly what I did

I thought of joining the service
I really wanted that
But I was a single parent
So that dream fell flat

I thought I'd write a book
I'm really pretty smart
Once I picked up the pen,
Couldn't think of where to start

I dream of hope
I dream of ambition
I dream of the power
To make a good decision

*There's so many things*
*I thought I could be*
*Never once in my life*
*I thought I'd be free*

*I'm glad I can laugh*
*Sometimes I might cry*
*Sometimes I may scream*
*And ask Lord God why??!!*

*Today in my life*
*I'm able to dream*
*My life's not as bad*
*As it may seem..*

# Talent

I don't exercise
I don't run
I tried to do a pushup
But it wasn't so much fun

I can't draw a picture
Not really my skill
My talent is poetry
With that I get a thrill

I'm able to express myself
In words I never thought
Take me to deeper places
Places I never sought

I have no ear for music
My voice sounds quite flat
Dancing's not my thing
I'm very sure of that

Poetry is unwinding
Poetry sets me free
Poetry I my own words
Poetry releases me..

# That Look on Your Face

*I sat in that chair*
*Pouring out my soul*
*Hurting inside*
*I didn't have a goal*

*What did I want?*
*What was I working for?*
*I want my recovery*
*And it's not outside that door*

*I bawled a little bit*
*But that was ok*
*That's why I came to you*
*To show me the way*

*To help me get through*
*To work out my pain*
*One day I promise*
*These tears will rain*

*I vented frustration*
*I thought I was angry*
*When I turned my head*
*I looked quite strangely*

Up in the window
I saw your face
My voice got quiet
My heart started to race

That look you had
It made my heart drop
Right in midsentence
Did all my words stop

As I stared at you,
You opened the door
I didn't know what to say
So I stared at the floor

You both talked to me
You worked as a team
You explained to me
What my feelings mean

You told me I was loved
You said I was important
You told me my thoughts
Were all kinds of distorted

*I am making progress*
*That much I am sure*
*I'll never forget*
*How I felt secure*

*There's one thing*
*I could never erase*
*And that's that look*
*You had on your face*

# I Applaud You

I applaud you for your care
I applaud you for your concern
I applaud you for who you are
And your ability to discern

I applaud you for your thinking
I applaud you for your stance
I applaud you because you believe
That everyone deserves a chance

I applaud you for your knowledge
I applaud you for your degree
I applaud you for helping others
I applaud you for helping me

I applaud you for your wisdom
I applaud you for your sympathy
I applaud you for your remorse
I applaud you for your empathy

I applaud you for understanding
I applaud you for your talks
I applaud you for your ability
To not sit around and balk

*I applaud you for being calm*
*I applaud you for being collected*
*I applaud you when you see*
*That someone's being neglected*

*I applaud you for your compassion*
*I applaud you for your pride*
*I applaud you for staying*
*And not pushing us aside*

*I applaud your ability to be sincere*
*I applaud your willingness not to tell*
*I applaud that smile that comes on your face*
*Every time you hear "Ms. Michele"*

*I applaud you for your metaphors*
*I applaud you for your riddles*
*I applaud you for being honest*
*I applaud you for being "Ms. Criddle"*

# *Fly Me to the Moon...*

*Fly me to the moon*
*And take me now away*
*Wherever you go,*
*I promise I will stay*
*I shall walk among the craters*
*To see the North Star*
*I shall only look upon the Earth*
*Out here from afar*
*To sit on the surface*
*With our hands on our knees*
*Watching the earth turn*
*Watch the many seas*
*Wondering about the people*
*We left behind that day*
*We had no other choice*
*There was no other way*
*For us to be alone*
*In the quietness and still*
*Are we ever coming back?*
*I'm sure that we will*
*Not today, not tomorrow*
*I'm not really sure when*
*Whenever we find out*
*You'll know by then*
*In the meantime,*
*We must sit & enjoy the scene*
*Watching the beautiful Saturn spin*

*Oh, how serene*
*As I look into your eyes*
*You into mine*
*In my corner vision*
*The sun begins to shine*
*It twinkles in your eye*
*Sparkles in the other*
*The Sun was my father*
*The Moon was my mother*
*Long lost loves*
*Now an eternity apart*
*It's over for them*
*For us it's a start*
*There's no place in the entire Galaxy*
*I'd rather be*
*No one I'd rather love*
*As far as my eyes can see...*

# Meditation

This one big tree
With branches out wide
Stands alone
In all of outside

I look at that tree
So great and tall
As one little leaf
Begins to fall

While the tree contrasted
Against the afternoon sky
I think to myself
Just who am I?

I wish I could lie
Up under that tree
And think of the ways
That I love me

I looked at the clouds
As they're grey and big
A Blue Jay perches
On a little twig

*It stays for a minute*
*Before it's off again*
*I'm sure it'll be back*
*I just don't know when*

*I wish I could be*
*Like that bird & that leaf*
*I might dream about it*
*When I go to sleep*

*For I may fall*
*But I will not stay*
*I'll get up, dust off*
*And find another way.*

# Free

As the birds chirp
And the flowers bloom
As the sun rises
And the wind blows
Every morning I stretch
And open my eyes

I realize I'm free

As my breaths come and go
And my walk is steady
As I take in my sights
And be thankful for all I have
As I smile my biggest smile
And laugh as loud as I can

I realize I'm free

Things could be worse
But they are not
I could be gone
But I am not
I could give up
But I will not

Because I am free.

# Special Thanks

*Santa Maria*

*There's a place you can go*
*If you made a mistake*
*If your life was unmanageable*
*This is a place that will take*

*You with open arms*
*With plenty of hugs*
*Lots of understanding*
*And will not judge*

*This is a place that I've been*
*I have learned so much*
*From not doing drugs*
*To knowing a gentle touch*

*See, when I first came*
*To Jacquelyn Street*
*I couldn't say anything*
*For I was in defeat*

*I was skeptical of others*
*Cautious of what I'd say*
*Sad that I was there*
*Didn't want to get in the way*

*Eventually I did talk*
*Then you couldn't shut me up*
*I would talk and talk and talk*
*But I was no longer stuck*

*Sitting in groups all day*
*Relearning how to live*
*Saying to myself*
*Something's got to give*

*People telling me what to do*
*Trust me, I hated that*
*As much as I wanted to leave*
*In those chairs my behind sat*

*So to Ms. Michele, Coach Lanisha,*
*Ms. Cindy, and Ms. Kim,*
*To Ms. Shannon, and Ms. Lucia,*
*And all the rest of them*

*I want to just say thank you*
*For opening up your door*
*I know you'll always have room*
*For many, many more!*

# Acknowledgements

*First and foremost, I want to thank God and His Son, Jesus Christ for making me and for giving me this beautiful gift of poetry. Secondly, I want to thank my mother because without her truly none of this would have been possible. I want to thank all of my friends from Santa Maria Hostel in Houston, TX: Jaime S., Jill B., Candice G., Michelle (Rhianon)., Angela C., Brittany C., Special thanks to Kellye M. I love you friend. Patsy P., Kanteeza, Emily B., Amber G., Trisha G., Lupita S., I love you Casey B., Ambroseanda, Michelle M., Liz S., Mallory P., Mona D., Love you so much Kara T., Rebekah B., Kenisha C., Briana S. you go girl, Lindsey B., Kim K., Lesley W., Charmaine M., Jenifer R., Amber M., Porcha B.. We are bound together here in this book. I owe so much gratitude to the Santa Maria staff: Ms.Eartha, Ms. Angela, and Ms. Amanda. To Ms. Frankie, Ms. Tiffany, Ms. C, and Ms. Lee, you all have remained patient with me when I had hard times. Thank you. Last but certainly not least, to all of the counselors: Ms. Michele, words cannot explain how I feel about everything you have done for me. You have shown me how to live and for that I am eternally grateful. You will make an indent on so many people's lives. My heart swells at how much patience you have shown me. Thank you is nowhere near enough to say to you. Ms. Lucia, you were always an open door for me. You would stop what you were doing to just listen to me. You gave me the courage to write this book. Thank you. Ms. Shannon. Hey! Ms. Shannon, you were the best person to come and talk to when I needed someone to talk to. I came in a wreck and left feeling a ton better and you never even said a word. I also want to thank you for encouraging me to write* a rebuttal to "Enemy". You truly are a miracle worker. Ms. Cindy, although I never talked to you one on one, the way you taught groups were amazing. You had a way of making three hour groups seem like twenty minutes. Watching you sing the Santa Maria song was nothing short of a concert! Coach Lanisha, although you had a way with language in your group, you took your group serious. Anyone could clearly see how passionate you are with your recovery. Ms. Kim, so very fashionable you were! The most stylish counselor there was. Oh! I couldn't possibly forget Ms. Amber! You made treatment feel like a happy place. Every treatment facility needs you Ms. Amber! You laughed with us, cried with us and were strict when need...as much as you could be. I hope one day we can race again, maybe this time you will win. I can think of one more person to thank and that's my dear friend Carlos, who let me use his WiFi to complete this book. I love all of ya'll

-Yvonne S.